Simplifying Success:The marketing Mastery code

Johnathan A. Barnes

- Navigating Technological Disruptions in Marketing

CHAPTER 9
- Beyond Mastery: Innovations and Trends
- AI and Automation in Marketing
- Emerging Trends Shaping the Future of Marketing

Conclusion

INTRODUCTION

Decoding Marketing Mastery

In today's interconnected world, the realm of marketing has evolved into an intricate tapestry of creativity, strategy, and technological innovation. The term "Decoding Marketing Mastery" encapsulates the essence of unraveling the intricate layers of this dynamic field, where marketers strive to combine artistry and data-driven insights to captivate audiences and drive business success. This introduction delves into the key components that define marketing mastery, shedding light on the art and science that underpin its practice.

At its core, marketing mastery encompasses the profound ability to decipher consumer behavior, market trends, and emerging technologies to formulate strategies that resonate with audiences. Gone are the days of one-size-fits-all advertising; the modern marketer is a skilled decoder, meticulously translating customer insights into tailored messages and experiences. This process involves understanding the intricacies of human psychology, analyzing demographic data, and staying attuned to cultural shifts. The art of decoding these nuanced cues empowers marketers to create campaigns that not only engage but also establish emotional connections with consumers.

Yet, marketing in the digital age extends beyond intuition and artistic flair. Mastery in this field demands a profound understanding of the science underpinning consumer interactions. The advent of advanced analytics, big data, and artificial intelligence has ushered in an era where data-driven decision-making reigns supreme. Marketers must adeptly navigate through complex metrics, interpreting click-through rates, conversion funnels, and engagement analytics to fine-tune their campaigns. This fusion of creativity and data science yields a potent combination, allowing campaigns to be agile and responsive to ever-changing market dynamics.

Decoding marketing mastery also involves navigating the intricate web of digital platforms that have revolutionized how brands connect with their audience. Social media, search engines, and e-commerce platforms have become virtual marketplaces where businesses compete for attention. Understanding the algorithms that dictate content visibility, mastering search engine optimization techniques, and harnessing the power of influencer marketing are all pivotal elements in this pursuit. The mastery lies in leveraging these platforms to craft seamless, omnichannel experiences that guide consumers effortlessly along their journey from awareness to purchase.

In the age of information overload, crafting a compelling narrative is another hallmark of marketing mastery. Storytelling transcends mere product promotion; it involves weaving a captivating narrative that resonates with the audience's aspirations, values, and desires.

Skillful marketers know that a well-told story has the potential to etch a brand into the collective consciousness, making it more than a product and transforming it into a lifestyle or an ideology. Decoding marketing mastery involves identifying the threads of emotion, conflict, and resolution that resonate with consumers and infusing them into brand narratives that leave an indelible mark.

While decoding marketing mastery encompasses a multitude of skills, its ultimate goal is to drive tangible business outcomes. The modern marketer is no longer just a creative mind; they are a revenue generator, a growth driver, and a strategic partner to the organization. This mastery requires a keen understanding of ROI analysis, customer lifetime value, and the alignment of marketing goals with broader business objectives. By quantifying the impact of marketing initiatives, the marketer becomes a credible advocate for resource allocation, fostering a symbiotic relationship between creativity and the bottom line.

Decoding Marketing Mastery" encapsulates the art and science of modern marketing—a fusion of creativity, strategy, data science, and technological prowess. This introduction scratches the surface of the multifaceted world that marketers inhabit, where they decipher consumer behavior, orchestrate data-driven campaigns, navigate the digital landscape, craft compelling narratives, and drive business growth. As we delve deeper into the following chapters, the intricate layers of marketing mastery will be peeled away, revealing the strategies, tactics, and philosophies that empower brands to thrive in an ever-evolving marketplace.

CHAPTER 1
Understanding the Foundations of Marketing

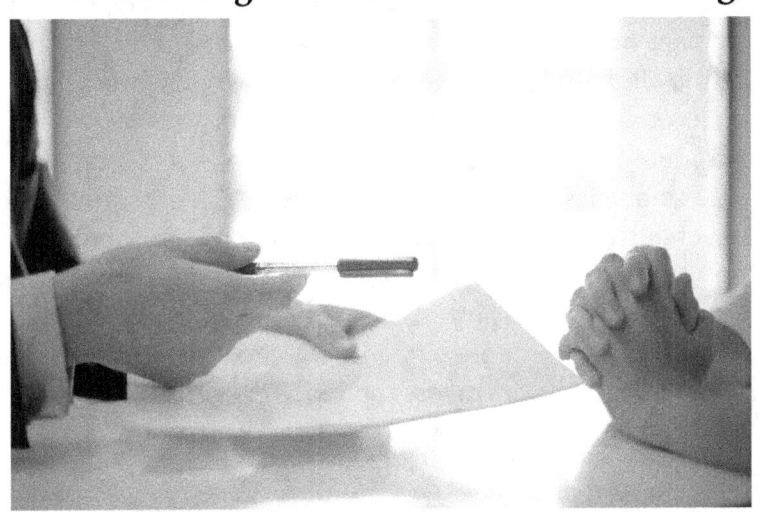

Marketing serves as the lifeblood of ultramodern business, playing a vital part in creating brand mindfulness, driving deals, and establishing strong client connections. To comprehend the intricate web of strategies, generalities, and principles that form the foundations of marketing, one must claw into its core factors client perceptivity, segmentation, targeting, positioning, the marketing blend, and the evolving digital geography. At the heart of effective marketing lies a deep understanding of client geste and preferences. client perceptivity, gathered through request exploration, checks, and data analysis, give the bedrock upon which successful marketing juggernauts are erected. By decoding the requirements, solicitations, and pain points of their target followership, businesses can conform their immolations to meet those specific demands. Segmentation, the process of dividing a miscellaneous request into distinct groups, is the posterior step. This acknowledges the diversity among consumers and acknowledges that a one- size- fits- all approach infrequently suffices. By relating common characteristics, similar as demographics, psychographics, and actions, marketers can produce parts that enable substantiated and reverberative messaging. Having established parts, the coming challenge is to choose the most promising groups to target. Targeting involves opting parts that align with the company's objects and coffers. The end is to pinpoint parts with a genuine need for the product or service and a advanced liability of conversion. This precise approach enhances the effectiveness of marketing sweats and optimizes resource allocation. Positioning, nearly intertwined with targeting, is how a brand defines its place in the minds of consumers relative to its challengers. It's about creating a unique and compelling value proposition that resonates with the target followership. Effective positioning establishes an emotional connection and sets the brand piecemeal in a crowded business. The marketing blend, frequently appertained to as the 4Ps product, price, place, and creation encompasses the politic rudiments of a marketing strategy. The product itself needs to address client requirements and wants, and its features, design, and quality play a pivotal part. Price, on the other hand, should align with the perceived value of the product and the target request's amenability to pay. Distribution channels(place) insure the product reaches the right consumers at the right time. Promotion involves the communication strategies that inform, convert, and remind consumers about the product's benefits. In the ultramodern period, the foundations of marketing have been significantly told by the digital revolution. The arrival of the internet, social media, ande-commerce has converted the way businesses interact with consumers. Digital marketing has enabled precise targeting, real-time engagement, and a wealth of data for analysis. Content marketing, social media advertising, hunt machine optimization, and influencer hookups have come vital tools in the marketer's magazine. likewise, the rise of consumer commission has shifted the dynamics. The frequence of online reviews,stone generated content, and social sharing means that brands are now subject to public scrutiny like noway ahead. This necessitates authenticity, translucency, and a genuine commitment to client satisfaction. Understanding the foundations of marketing isn't simply an academic exercise; it's a critical skill for anyone involved in business, entrepreneurship, or indeed particular branding. client perceptivity, segmentation, targeting, positioning, the marketing blend, and digital engagement inclusively form the bedrock upon which successful marketing strategies are erected. As technology continues to evolve, so too will the styles and tools of marketing. Yet, the abecedarian principles of understanding and connecting with consumers will always remain at the core of this dynamic field.

Defining Marketing in Today's Landscape

In the ever- evolving geography of ultramodern business, the conception of marketing has converted from its traditional roots into a dynamic and multifaceted discipline. In moment's digital age, where technology, connectivity, and consumer geste are in a constant state of flux, the part of marketing has come more vital than ever ahead. This essay delves into the nuances of defining marketing in the contemporary geography, exploring its core principles, styles, and the challenges and openings it presents. At its core, marketing involves the strategic processes and conditioning aimed at creating, communicating, delivering, and swapping immolations that have value for guests, guests, mates, and society at large. While this description remains loyal, the tools, strategies, and channels employed by marketers have experienced a remarkable metamorphosis. The traditional 4Ps of marketing(Product, Price, Place, Promotion) have expanded to encompass new confines that reflect the ultramodern digital age. One of the most significant shifts in marketing has been the proliferation of digital platforms. The internet, social media, and mobile bias have revolutionized how businesses connect with their target cult. Online marketing has given rise to data- driven perceptivity, allowing marketers to understand consumer geste , preferences, and trends in unknown detail. This data- centric approach enables substantiated and largely targeted juggernauts, icing that the right communication reaches the right followership at the right time.   The conception of branding has also taken on a new dimension in the digital period. Branding is no longer confined to   ensigns and   taglines;   it encompasses the entire   client experience. moment's consumers seek authentic connections with brands that align with their values and bournes . This has urged companies to   concentrate on   erecting emotional connections and narratives that reverberate with their followership. Successful ultramodern brands stand for further than just their products; they embody a life and a purpose.   Social media platforms have come integral to ultramodern marketing strategies. These platforms grease direct relations between brands and consumers, blurring the lines between marketing and client service. Authentic engagement and meaningful dialogue are prized goods, as   guests decreasingly value translucency and responsiveness from the brands they support. Influencer marketing, a fairly recent miracle, leverages   individualities with substantial online entourages to plump products and services, staking on the trust established with their cult.   still, alongside these   openings, contemporary marketing faces challenges that are unique to the digital age. The information load brought about by the constant shower of online content poses a challenge for marketers seeking to capture and retain their   followership's attention. Standing out amidst the noise requires innovative and creative approaches that cut through the clutter and give genuine value.   also, the issue of sequestration and data security has come a critical concern. As companies collect and use vast quantities of client data, icing the ethical and responsible use of this information is consummate. Striking the right balance between personalization and esteeming sequestration is an ongoing challenge that marketers must navigate. The global nature of the digital geography has also broadened the midairs for marketing, taking an understanding of different societies, languages, and request nuances. Localization and artistic perceptivity have come essential considerations in casting effective marketing juggernauts for a global followership. dexterity and rigidity are crucial attributes for ultramodern marketers. The rapid-fire pace of technological advancements means that strategies and tactics must be flexible enough to evolve with the changing geography. Recession can lead to fustiness, making it imperative for marketers to embrace nonstop literacy and trial. Defining marketing in moment's geography requires a comprehensive understanding of its foundational principles and its elaboration in response to the digital age. The ultramodern marketer must blend creativity with data- driven perceptivity, fostering authentic connections with consumers through substantiated and applicable juggernauts. Challenges similar as information load, sequestration enterprises, and the need for artistic perceptivity accentuate the complex nature of ultramodern marketing. Yet, with these challenges come openings for invention, engagement, and growth. As long as businesses remain adaptable and married to understanding and serving their cult, marketing will continue to thrive as a driving force in the contemporary business realm.

The Role of Marketing in Business Success

Marketing, a fundamental component of any business strategy, plays a pivotal role in driving business success by connecting products or services with the right audience, fostering brand awareness, and ultimately influencing consumer behavior. In today's competitive landscape, effective marketing is not just a tool for growth, but a necessity for survival. This essay delves into the multifaceted role of marketing in achieving business success, highlighting its impact on customer engagement, brand establishment, and revenue generation.

At its core, marketing revolves around understanding customer needs and preferences. A successful business identifies its target audience and tailors its offerings to match their desires. Market research, a crucial aspect of marketing, enables businesses to gather insights into consumer behaviors, trends, and preferences. Armed with this information, companies can develop products or services that meet specific demands, thereby increasing the likelihood of success. Marketing research also aids in identifying gaps in the market and potential niches that can be exploited for competitive advantage.

Effective marketing goes beyond simply offering a product; it's about creating an emotional connection between the brand and the consumer. Branding, a central aspect of marketing, establishes a unique identity that resonates with customers. A well-defined brand identity not only differentiates a business from its competitors but also helps in establishing trust and loyalty among consumers. This emotional bond can translate into customer retention and advocacy, leading to sustained business success. A prime example is Apple, whose brand loyalty is fueled by its distinct identity and the aspirational lifestyle it represents.

Marketing acts as a bridge between the company and its customers. Through various channels, such as social media, advertising, and public relations, businesses can engage with their audience directly, creating a dialogue that fosters a sense of community. In the digital age, social media platforms have become invaluable tools for this purpose. Engaging content, interactive campaigns, and timely responses to customer inquiries not only enhance customer satisfaction but also increase the likelihood of referrals and positive word-of-mouth marketing.

In a globalized economy, where countless choices are available to consumers, visibility is key. Marketing ensures that businesses are visible and accessible to their target audience. Strategic advertising, whether through traditional mediums like television and print or modern channels like search engine optimization (SEO) and pay-per-click (PPC) advertising, increases a company's visibility and reach. An effective advertising campaign can create buzz around a product launch, attract new customers, and contribute to overall brand recognition.

Marketing drives revenue generation by stimulating demand for a company's products or services. Effective marketing campaigns not only attract new customers but also encourage existing customers to make repeat purchases. Pricing strategies, a subset of marketing, play a crucial role in revenue optimization. A well-thought-out pricing strategy takes into account factors such as production costs, competitor pricing, and perceived value to strike a balance between profitability and customer affordability. Discounts, promotions, and bundling are examples of marketing tactics that can influence purchasing decisions and boost sales.

The digital era has transformed the marketing landscape, introducing new avenues and challenges. Online marketing, including social media marketing, content marketing, and influencer partnerships, has gained prominence due to its cost-effectiveness and extensive reach. However, the rapid pace of technological advancements also means that businesses need to adapt continuously to stay relevant. Search algorithms change, consumer behaviors evolve, and new platforms emerge, necessitating agile marketing strategies that can pivot swiftly.

The role of marketing in business success is multidimensional and far-reaching. From understanding customer needs through market research to creating emotional connections through branding and engaging customers through various channels, marketing is a driving force behind business growth. The relationship between marketing and revenue generation underscores its significance in achieving financial success. In an increasingly competitive and dynamic business environment, a robust marketing strategy is not a luxury, but a prerequisite for any business aiming to thrive. As markets continue to evolve, businesses that prioritize innovation and creativity in their marketing efforts are poised to reap the rewards of sustained success.

CHAPTER 2

Unveiling the Mastery Code

In a world driven by constant change and evolving challenges, the pursuit of mastery is a dateless bid. The mastery law represents the admixture of principles, practices, and perspectives that enable individualities to reach their loftiest situations of performance and achievement. It's a roadmap to unleashing mortal eventuality, fostering particular growth, and attaining excellence in any field. The trip to unveil this law requires tone- discovery, perseverance, and an unyielding commitment to growth. At its core, the mastery law revolves around the idea of deliberate practice a conception innovated by psychologist Anders Ericsson. Deliberate practice involves violent, focused, and purposeful trouble aimed at perfecting specific chops. It demands stepping out of the comfort zone, embracing challenges, and continuously enriching one's capacities. This practice isn't about careless reiteration, but rather about strategic reiteration with a clear end to correct miscalculations, enhance ways, and elevate performance. Central to the mastery law is the growth mindset, a conception developed by psychologist Carol Dweck. This mindset emphasizes the belief that capacities and intelligence can be developed through fidelity and hard work. Those who retain a growth mindset view failures as openings for literacy and lapses as stepping monuments toward enhancement. Cultivating a growth mindset empowers individualities to embrace challenges with enthusiasm, persist in the face of adversity, and eventually unleash their full eventuality. Another essential hand of the mastery law is the conception of" inflow," introduced by psychologist Mihaly Csikszentmihalyi. Flow is a state of deep engagement and optimal performance where individualities are completely absorbed in an exertion. Achieving inflow requires chancing the delicate balance between challenge and skill – too important challenge leads to anxiety, while too little challenge leads to tedium. When in inflow, time seems to vanish, and individualities witness a sense of heightened focus, creativity, and satisfaction. The mastery law is also intricately linked to the principle of deliberate rest. In a society that glorifies busyness, taking time to rest and recharge is frequently overlooked. still, studies show that deliberate rest is essential for cognitive revivification, creativity, and sustained performance. Incorporating ages of rest, relaxation, and reflection into bone's routine can lead to enhanced productivity, internal clarity, and overall well- being. In the pursuit of mastery, mentorship and feedback play vital places. Connecting with instructors who have formerly traveled the path to mastery can give inestimable perceptivity, guidance, and lanes. Formative feedback from instructors, peers, and indeed tone- assessment is pivotal for relating areas of enhancement and refining bone's approach. Embracing a growth- acquainted station toward feedback creates a nonstop cycle of literacy and refinement. also, the mastery law requires a commitment to lifelong literacy. In a fleetly changing world, recession is the adversary of mastery. Cultivating a thirst for knowledge, seeking out new gests , and conforming to arising trends are vital for staying ahead of the wind. The amenability to evolve and learn from different sources fosters rigidity, invention, and a broader perspective. While the mastery law provides a design for particular development, it isn't without its challenges. prostrating tone- mistrustfulness, fear of failure, and the temptation to settle for mediocrity are all hurdles on the path to mastery. It demands adaptability, tone- discipline, and the capability to persist in the face of lapses. still, these challenges are integral to the growth process and contribute to the development of strength, character, and a jacked sense of accomplishment. Unveiling the Mastery Code is an disquisition of the principles and practices that empower individualities to reach their loftiest eventuality. It encompasses deliberate practice, a growth mindset, achieving inflow, deliberate rest, mentorship, feedback, lifelong literacy, and prostrating challenges. By embracing these rudiments, individualities can embark on a transformative trip toward particular excellence and mastery in their chosen fields. The mastery law serves as a memorial that greatness isn't a destination but a nonstop pursuit a trip of tone- discovery, growth, and the consummation of mortal eventuality.

The Five Pillars of Marketing Mastery

Marketing Mastery is an essential concept that encapsulates the art and science of effective marketing strategies. It involves a deep understanding of consumer behavior, market dynamics, and innovative techniques to create a lasting impact. The Five Pillars of Marketing Mastery serve as the foundation for achieving excellence in the field, combining both traditional and modern approaches.

1. Market Research and Analysis:

At the core of Marketing Mastery lies the ability to conduct comprehensive market research and analysis. This pillar involves understanding consumer needs, preferences, and behaviors. Effective market research uncovers insights into target demographics, competitive landscapes, and emerging trends. Armed with this knowledge, marketers can tailor their strategies to resonate with their audience, anticipate market shifts, and capitalize on new opportunities.

2. Strategic Branding:

Building a strong brand presence is another vital pillar of Marketing Mastery. Strategic branding goes beyond a mere logo; it encompasses a brand's identity, values, and messaging. Successful branding creates an emotional connection with consumers, fostering loyalty and advocacy. A well-defined brand strategy ensures consistency across all touchpoints, whether online or offline, and helps the brand stand out in a crowded marketplace.

3. Compelling Content Creation:

In the digital age, content is king. The third pillar of Marketing Mastery focuses on creating compelling and valuable content that resonates with the target audience. Whether it's blog posts, social media updates, videos, or podcasts, high-quality content establishes a brand's authority and builds trust. Content should be relevant, engaging, and tailored to meet the needs of the audience, contributing to brand awareness and customer engagement.

4. Multichannel Marketing:

With the proliferation of digital platforms, multichannel marketing has become a cornerstone of Marketing Mastery. This pillar involves identifying and leveraging the most suitable channels to reach the target audience effectively. From social media and email marketing to search engine optimization and influencer collaborations, a well-executed multichannel approach ensures that the brand's message reaches customers where they are most active.

5. Data-Driven Decision Making:

The final pillar of Marketing Mastery centers around data-driven decision making. In the modern landscape, access to data and analytics provides invaluable insights into campaign performance and customer behavior. Marketers adept in this pillar utilize key performance indicators (KPIs) to measure success, optimize strategies based on real-time data, and make informed decisions that drive ROI. A constant feedback loop between analysis and action ensures continuous improvement and adaptability.

The Five Pillars of Marketing Mastery form a holistic framework for achieving excellence in the ever-evolving field of marketing. Market research and analysis lay the foundation by understanding consumer needs and market dynamics. Strategic branding creates a distinct identity that resonates with the audience. Compelling content creation fosters engagement and authority. Multichannel marketing ensures a wider reach, while data-driven decision making guides strategies for optimal results.

By mastering these pillars, marketers gain a competitive edge in today's dynamic business landscape, enabling them to navigate complexities and deliver impactful campaigns that drive brand growth and customer loyalty. Marketing Mastery is an ongoing journey, requiring a blend of creativity, strategic thinking, and adaptability to stay ahead in an ever-changing environment.

CHAPTER 3

Target Audience Identification

In the ever-evolving landscape of marketing, the concept of target audience identification stands as a foundational pillar upon which successful campaigns are built. It is the art and science of identifying, understanding, and segmenting the audience that is most likely to resonate with a product, service, or message. In a world of diverse preferences and interests, businesses and marketers are challenged to navigate through the noise and deliver tailored content that captivates the right individuals. This article delves into the significance, methods, challenges, and benefits of target audience identification, shedding light on how this process shapes modern marketing strategies.

The Significance of Target Audience Identification:
In an era of information overload, capturing the attention of potential customers has become an arduous task. This is where target audience identification becomes a strategic imperative. It enables marketers to direct their efforts and resources toward individuals who are not only interested in their offerings but are also more likely to convert into loyal customers. By understanding the demographics, psychographics, behaviors, and pain points of their audience, businesses can create messaging that resonates, leading to higher engagement rates, improved customer satisfaction, and enhanced brand loyalty.

Methods of Target Audience Identification:

Effective target audience identification is not a shot in the dark; it's a meticulously crafted process. Market research plays a pivotal role, employing both qualitative and quantitative techniques. Surveys, focus groups, interviews, and social media monitoring provide insights into consumer preferences and opinions. Demographic information, such as age, gender, location, and income, helps refine the audience's scope. Psychographic data, encompassing interests, values, and lifestyle choices, paints a more vivid picture of consumer behavior. Moreover, data analytics and tracking tools assist in deciphering online behavior, aiding in the identification of potential customers.

Challenges in Target Audience Identification:

While the benefits are clear, identifying a target audience is not without its challenges. The modern consumer is complex and multifaceted, making it difficult to predict their responses accurately. Market trends shift rapidly, requiring marketers to stay updated with the latest shifts in consumer preferences. Additionally, there's the risk of overgeneralizing or stereotyping the audience, leading to misguided marketing efforts. Balancing the use of data analytics with ethical considerations about consumer privacy is also a persistent concern.

Benefits of Target Audience Identification:

The rewards of precise target audience identification are manifold. A well-defined audience allows for the creation of tailor-made content, resulting in higher engagement rates and more effective conversions. It optimizes resource allocation by preventing wastage on broad-reaching strategies that might not resonate with the intended consumers. A deep understanding of the audience's pain points and desires empowers marketers to position their offerings as solutions, enhancing brand credibility. Over time, this process builds stronger relationships, leading to repeat business and word-of-mouth referrals.

Evolution with Technological Advancements:

The digital age has revolutionized the way target audience identification is approached. Advanced algorithms and machine learning tools analyze massive datasets to uncover patterns and behaviors that were previously inconceivable. Social media platforms, with their vast user base and detailed user profiles, provide unparalleled insights into audience preferences. Automation further streamlines the process, enabling real-time adjustments based on the effectiveness of ongoing campaigns. However, the human touch remains irreplaceable, as emotional nuances and context often require a nuanced understanding.

Personalization and Customization:

In an era where consumers are bombarded with information, personalization has become the holy grail of marketing. Target audience identification fuels this personalization engine by allowing businesses to craft messages that resonate on an individual level. Tailored recommendations, exclusive offers, and relevant content create a sense of connection and belonging. This leads to higher engagement rates, increased brand loyalty, and a stronger likelihood of advocacy. Customization goes beyond demographics, delving into the intricacies of consumer behaviors and preferences.

The Intersection of Ethics and Identification:
As technology advances, concerns about privacy, data usage, and ethical considerations loom large. Collecting and utilizing consumer data require responsible practices to ensure compliance with regulations and respect for user privacy.

Navigating Market Segmentation

Request segmentation is a abecedarian conception in ultramodern marketing that involves dividing a broad consumer request into lower, more manageable parts grounded on participated characteristics, requirements, and actions. This strategic approach allows businesses to conform their marketing sweats to specific groups, leading to further effective communication and advanced client satisfaction. Navigating request segmentation involves a multifaceted process that includes understanding its significance, relating segmentation variables, developing target parts, and enforcing acclimatized strategies. request segmentation is pivotal because it recognizes the essential diversity within a large request. Consumers aren't homogenous; they've varying preferences, actions, and copping habits. trying to target the entire request with a single communication or product is frequently ineffective, as it fails to reverberate with individual consumer requirements. By segmenting the request, businesses can address these different requirements in a further targeted manner. The first step in navigating request segmentation is relating applicable variables that can be used to separate consumer groups. These variables can be astronomically distributed into demographic, psychographic, behavioral, and geographic factors. Demographic variables include age, gender, income, education, and family size. Psychographic variables claw into consumers' cultures, values, interests, and personality traits. Behavioral variables consider copping patterns, brand fidelity, operation frequence, and benefits sought. Geographic variables take into account the physical position of consumers. Once segmentation variables are established, the coming phase involves segmenting the request. This involves grouping consumers with analogous characteristics together to produce distinct parts. The challenge lies in chancing a balance between creating parts that are too broad to be meaningful and parts that are too narrow to be feasible. The parts should be substantial enough to warrant targeted marketing sweats, but also distinct enough to have unique requirements. After segmenting the request, businesses must elect target parts. This decision is grounded on factors similar as the member's size, growth eventuality, attractiveness, and comity with the association's coffers and capabilities. Not all parts will be inversely precious to a business, so careful consideration is demanded to determine which parts align stylish with the company's pretensions and strengths. With target parts linked, the coming phase involves developing acclimatized marketing strategies for each member. This requires an in- depth understanding of the member's characteristics, requirements, and preferences. dispatches, products, pricing, distribution channels, and promotional conditioning should all be customized to reverberate with the specific member. This personalization enhances consumer engagement and fidelity, leading to bettered business issues. An essential tool in navigating request segmentation is request exploration. Effective request exploration provides businesses with precious perceptivity into consumer actions and preferences. ways similar as checks, focus groups, and data analysis can help upgrade segmentation variables, validate target parts, and fine- tune marketing strategies. Regularly streamlined request exploration ensures that businesses remain attuned to evolving consumer trends and demands. Segmentation does not solely profit businesses; it also enhances the consumer experience. When consumers admit dispatches and immolations that align with their preferences, they're more likely to engage with the brand and come pious guests. This collective benefit forms the foundation of long- term connections between businesses and consumers. In practice, successful request segmentation requires ongoing evaluation and adaptation. Consumer actions and preferences change over time, challenging nonstop refinement of segmentation variables and strategies. Regular feedback circles, analysis of deals data, and monitoring of request trends enable businesses to acclimatize and respond effectively to changing dynamics. Navigating request segmentation is a multifaceted process that plays a vital part in ultramodern marketing strategies. By dividing a miscellaneous request into distinct parts grounded on participated characteristics and preferences, businesses can conform their sweats for maximum impact. relating segmentation variables, developing target parts, and enforcing substantiated strategies are all integral way in this process. request exploration serves as a guiding tool, furnishing perceptivity into consumer actions and abetting in strategy development. Eventually, successful request segmentation enhances both business issues and consumer gests, pressing its significance in moment's competitive geography.

Crafting Customer Personas for Precision

In the fleetly evolving geography of ultramodern business, understanding your guests has come consummate. Gone are the days when generalized marketing strategies could serve. moment, perfection is the name of the game, and casting accurate client personas is the key to unleashing success. client personas are detailed and semi-fictional representations of your ideal guests, erected upon thorough exploration and analysis. By probing deep into the psyche of your target followership, you can conform your products, services, and marketing sweats to reverberate with them on a particular position. This composition explores the process of casting client personas for perfection and delves into why they're pivotal for driving business growth.

Understanding the Significance

client personas serve as a compass guiding your business opinions. They give perceptivity into your guests' provocations, pain points, preferences, and actions. This information allows you to develop products that feed to their requirements, produce marketing juggernauts that speak to their solicitations, and establish a brand identity that resonates with their values. In a request impregnated with choices, casting client personas offers a competitive edge by enabling you to cut through the noise and directly engage with your target followership.

Research and Data Collection

The foundation of perfection in casting client personas lies in scrupulous exploration and data collection. Start by assaying being client data, conducting checks, and exercising analytics tools to gain perceptivity into client geste. Explore demographics, psychographics, and buying patterns. Social media platforms, online forums, and client feedback are goldmines for understanding client sentiment, pain points, and bournes . also, canvassing current guests and implicit leads can give precious firsthand perceptivity into their preferences and challenges.

Segmentation

Not all guests are the same, and casting a single persona won't serve. Segmentation involves dividing your client base into distinct groups grounded on participated characteristics. This allows for the creation of personas that directly represent each member. For case, a apparel brand might member its guests grounded on factors like age, gender, life, and shopping habits. By understanding the unique traits of each member, you can conform your messaging and immolations to feed to their specific requirements.

Developing Persona Biographies

Once you've gathered sufficient data and segmented your followership, it's time to develop detailed persona biographies. A persona should be further than just a name and a stock print; it should come to life as a relatable existent. Give your persona a name, age, occupation, family status, and other applicable demographic details. Go beyond demographics and claw into their bournes , challenges, provocations, and values. Understand their preferred communication channels, content consumption habits, and copping geste. The further comprehensive the persona, the better you can understand and connect with your followership.

Confirmation and Refinement

Creating personas isn't a one- time task. Regular confirmation and refinement are pivotal to keeping them accurate and effective. As your business evolves and the request changes, client preferences and actions will shift. Periodically readdress and modernize your personas to insure they reflect the current reality. Collect feedback from your deals and client service brigades to identify any disagreement between your personas and the factual client relations they witness.

Impact on Business Strategy

Precision- drafted client personas have a profound impact on your business strategy. They guide product development by pressing features that align with client requirements. They inform marketing sweats by acclimatizing dispatches that reverberate with the feelings and provocations of your followership. Deals brigades can use personas to epitomize their relations and address client pain points effectively. also, personas aid in relating new openings and niches within your request, allowing you to pivot or expand strategically.

Real- world Success Stories

multitudinous companies have reaped the benefits of perfection- drafted client personas. Airbnb, for illustration, created a persona named" Sarah," who represented a solo rubberneck looking for unique and budget-friendly lodgment . This persona guided their platform's design and marketing sweats, leading to remarkable success. HubSpot, a marketing and deals platform, developed personas grounded on assiduity places and challenges, allowing them to knitter content and results to specific pain points. These success stories illustrate the power of personas in driving growth and applicability.

CHAPTER 4
Compelling Branding Strategies

In the ever- evolving geography of ultramodern business, branding has surfaced as a important tool for companies seeking to sculpt a unique identity and reverberate with their target followership. Effective branding strategies extend far beyond ensigns and color schemes; they synopsize a company's values, pledge, and personality, creating a lasting connection with consumers. In a request swamped with choices, compelling branding strategies have come the linchpin that differentiates successful companies from the rest. At the core of any compelling branding strategy lies a deep understanding of the target followership. request exploration and consumer perceptivity serve as the foundation upon which all other branding rudiments are erected. A company that comprehends its guests' requirements, preferences, and bournes gains a competitive edge by acclimatizing its branding to align with these factors. By fastening on the emotional triggers that drive copping opinions, businesses can draft a brand narrative that resonates on a particular position. thickness is a foundation of effective branding. A compelling brand should present a unified communication across all touchpoints from announcements and social media to packaging and client service. This thickness builds trust and reinforces the brand's identity in the minds of consumers. Apple, for case, is a high illustration of a company that has learned thickness in branding, with its minimalist design, stoner-friendly interfaces, and unwavering focus on invention. liar is a potent tool that transcends societies and generations, making it an integral part of compelling branding strategies. Brands that can tell a witching story about their origins, values, or impact on the world can forge an emotional connection that goes beyond deals. Patagonia, an out-of-door apparel company, exemplifies this approach by weaving stories of environmental activism into its brand narrative, reverberating with consumers who partake its values. Rigidity is pivotal in a fast- paced request. Compelling branding strategies aren't stationary; they evolve to stay applicable and fresh. This requires a amenability to embrace change and, at times, indeed resuscitate the brand. Nike's" Just Do It" watchword, for case, has seamlessly acclimated over the times to encompass a range of meanings, from particular commission to social justice advocacy, icing the brand remains culturally applicable. Authenticity is the bedrock on which trust is erected. Consumers moment can fluently discern insincere marketing sweats, and a lack of authenticity can lead to brand corrosion. Successful brands remain true to their core values, demonstrating translucency and honesty. Dove's" Real Beauty" crusade, which celebrates diversity and challenges conventional beauty norms, has reverberated with consumers due to its genuine commitment to promoting tone- confidence. In the digital age, an online presence is non-negotiable. Compelling branding strategies influence digital platforms to engage with guests in real-time, creating a two- way dialogue. Social media, blogs, and podcasts enable brands to partake precious content, respond to client inquiries, and humanize the brand by showcasing its people and processes. Wendy's facetious and interactive Twitter presence is a high illustration of using digital channels to establish a unique brand voice and connect with guests. Collaborations can fit new life into a brand by tapping into reciprocal requests or influencers. Partnering with another brand or a well- admired figure can introduce a brand to new cult and advance it credibility. The collaboration between Adidas and Kanye West, performing in the Yeezy line of lurkers, demonstrates how a strategic cooperation can lead to immense success by incorporating fashion, music, and celebrity influence. Creating a sense of belonging can foster brand fidelity. When consumers feel like they're part of a community or movement, their emotional investment in the brand deepens. Harley- Davidson, for illustration, has cultivated a pious following by situating its brand as a symbol of rebellion and fellowship, fostering a sense of belonging among its guests. Compelling branding strategies are the compass that guides companies through the complications of the ultramodern business. They go beyond face- position aesthetics and dive into the emotional and cerebral realm, forging connections that transcend deals. By understanding their followership, remaining harmonious, telling authentic stories, embracing change, and using digital platforms, brands can produce a important identity that stands out in a ocean of choices. Through strategic collaborations and a focus on erecting communities, brands can foster fidelity that withstands the test of time. In a world where isolation is crucial, the art of compelling branding remains a foundation of business success.

The Power of a Strong Brand Identity

A strong brand identity is an invaluable asset that wields considerable influence over a company's success and reputation. It encompasses more than just a logo and color scheme; it encompasses the entirety of a brand's visual and verbal communication, creating a cohesive and resonant experience for consumers. This power to evoke emotions, establish loyalty, and differentiate from competitors makes a robust brand identity an essential tool for businesses to thrive in today's competitive landscape.

At its core, a brand identity serves as a visual representation of a company's values, mission, and personality. It conveys a message even before a single word is spoken, eliciting emotions and associations that shape consumers' perceptions. Consider the iconic Apple logo a simple, sleek apple with a clean bite taken out of it. This logo immediately conjures notions of innovation, simplicity, and elegance. It is a testament to the power of a well-crafted brand identity to encapsulate complex ideas into a single, recognizable symbol.

Beyond the visual elements, a strong brand identity harmonizes all aspects of a company's communication, fostering consistency and coherence. This consistency builds credibility and trust over time, as consumers come to rely on a certain level of quality associated with the brand. Think about Nike's tagline, "Just Do It." These three words have become synonymous with perseverance, determination, and athletic achievement. By consistently using this tagline across their marketing efforts, Nike has reinforced their brand's message and mission, creating a lasting impact on consumers.

A robust brand identity has the power to evoke strong emotional connections with consumers. Human beings are inherently emotional creatures, and successful branding taps into these emotions. Coca-Cola, for instance, doesn't just sell a beverage; it sells happiness, togetherness, and nostalgia. Its brand identity, characterized by the iconic red and white color scheme and the elegant script font, transports consumers to a world of shared moments and warm feelings. This emotional resonance fosters brand loyalty, leading consumers to choose Coca-Cola not merely out of necessity, but out of a desire to be part of the brand's narrative.

In a crowded marketplace, differentiation is key, and a strong brand identity provides a competitive edge. Consider the luxury automobile manufacturer, Mercedes-Benz. Its brand identity is synonymous with sophistication, engineering excellence, and prestige. By consistently portraying these values, Mercedes-Benz distinguishes itself from other car manufacturers and creates a sense of exclusivity that attracts a specific target audience willing to invest in the brand. This differentiation is not solely about the product; it's about the promise, the experience, and the lifestyle associated with the brand.

The power of a strong brand identity extends beyond consumer perceptions it can also affect a company's financial performance. Brands with a clear and compelling identity tend to command premium pricing. Consumers are often willing to pay more for products that align with their values and aspirations. This willingness to pay a premium contributes to enhanced profitability and a healthier bottom line. For example, Starbucks has built a brand identity around the experience of savoring premium coffee in a cozy, welcoming environment. This has allowed them to charge premium prices compared to other coffee chains.

A well-defined brand identity facilitates brand extensions and diversification. When consumers have a strong positive association with a brand, they are more likely to explore new offerings from that brand with an open mind. This versatility can lead to expanded market presence and revenue streams. Take Disney as an example. Originally known for its animated films, Disney's strong brand identity allowed it to successfully expand into theme parks, merchandise, media networks, and even streaming services.

The power of a strong brand identity cannot be overstated. It goes beyond superficial aesthetics, shaping consumer perceptions, emotions, and behaviors. It builds trust, fosters loyalty, and differentiates a company in a competitive landscape. It resonates with audiences on an emotional level, creating a lasting bond that transcends mere transactions. Ultimately, a robust brand identity is an investment that yields significant returns, both in terms of financial success and the intangible value of a deeply ingrained presence in the hearts and minds of consumers.

Building Emotional Connections with Customers

In today's competitive business landscape, where products and services are often similar, building emotional connections with customers has emerged as a strategic imperative. Gone are the days when a transactional approach was sufficient to capture and retain customers. In the pursuit of long-term success, businesses must go beyond mere transactions and foster genuine emotional connections that resonate on a personal level.

The concept of emotional connection might seem intangible, but it holds immense power in shaping customer loyalty, brand perception, and overall business outcomes. It's about creating a bond that transcends the transactional nature of commerce and taps into the human aspects of relationships. This bond not only enhances customer satisfaction but also transforms them into brand advocates who willingly promote a company among their peers.

At the core of building emotional connections lies the principle of empathy. Understanding and addressing the needs, desires, and pain points of customers allows businesses to forge meaningful connections. When customers feel that a brand genuinely cares about them, they are more likely to develop a sense of loyalty and trust. This emotional resonance often arises from personalized interactions, where customers are treated as individuals rather than faceless consumers.

Storytelling is a powerful tool that businesses employ to create emotional connections. Sharing authentic stories about a company's origin, values, and impact can elicit an emotional response from customers. These stories humanize the brand, making it relatable and likable. Customers who connect with a brand's narrative on an emotional level are more likely to stick around and remain engaged over time.

Consistency is key when building emotional connections. Every touchpoint a customer has with a brand should reflect the same values, tone, and experience. Whether it's through customer service interactions, marketing campaigns, or product design, a consistent brand presence reinforces the emotional connection and builds familiarity.

Listening actively to customers plays a pivotal role in nurturing emotional connections. Soliciting feedback and actually implementing suggestions demonstrates that a brand values its customers' opinions. This not only enhances the customer's sense of ownership but also fosters a deeper emotional tie. Responding promptly and positively to customer concerns can turn a potentially negative situation into an opportunity to strengthen the connection.

Surprise and delight strategies can create memorable experiences that leave a lasting emotional impact. Going the extra mile to exceed customer expectations, whether through unexpected discounts, personalized thank-you notes, or exclusive offers, shows that a brand values its customers' loyalty. Such gestures resonate emotionally and are likely to be shared with others, amplifying the brand's reach.

Social media provides an ideal platform for building emotional connections. Engaging with customers on social media allows for real-time interactions, enabling brands to showcase their human side. Responding to comments, addressing queries, and sharing user-generated content demonstrate that a brand is present and interested in meaningful conversations. Additionally, leveraging social media to showcase behind-the-scenes glimpses and employee stories can create a sense of transparency and authenticity.

However, building emotional connections is not just a one-way street. Businesses must also connect emotionally with their employees. Employees who are proud of their company's values and culture are more likely to deliver exceptional customer experiences. When employees feel valued and connected, their enthusiasm and positivity trickle down to interactions with customers, further enhancing emotional bonds.

Building emotional connections with customers is a multifaceted endeavor that requires genuine empathy, consistency, storytelling, active listening, and personalization. These connections transcend transactional relationships, leading to increased customer loyalty, positive word-of-mouth, and brand advocacy. By treating customers as individuals and focusing on shared values and experiences, businesses can create lasting emotional connections that fuel long-term success in an increasingly competitive marketplace.

CHAPTER 5

Content that Captivate

Creating witching content is an art that combines creativity, strategy, and understanding your followership. To write content that truly captivates, you need to consider several crucial rudiments that engage compendiums , elicit feelings, and leave a continuing impact. This companion will give you with perceptivity and practicable tips to help you craft content that captivates your followership.

1. Understand Your followership

Before you start writing, it's pivotal to know your target followership. Research their preferences, interests, pain points, and demographics. conform your content to address their specific requirements, solicitations, and challenges.

2. Compelling Captions

Your caption is the first print compendiums have of your content. Craft attention- grabbing, clear, and terse captions that promise value, curiosity, or results. Use power words, figures, and questions to spark curiosity and encourage compendiums to claw deeper.

3. Hook with the preface

Your preface should hook compendiums and allure them to keep reading. Start with a witching yarn, a study- provoking question, a surprising statistic, or a relatable story that draws them in.

4. Give Value

insure your content offers genuine value to your followership. Whether it's educational, amusing, or perceptive, your content should fulfill a need or break a problem your compendiums have.

5. liar

Weaving stories into your content humanizes it and creates an emotional connection. Narratives reverberate deeply with compendiums , making your content memorable and relatable.

6. Visual Appeal

Incorporate illustrations similar as images, infographics, and vids to break up the textbook and enhance the visual appeal of your content. illustrations can help explain complex generalities and keep compendiums engaged.

7. Use Engaging Language

Employ pictorial and descriptive language that paints a picture in the anthology's mind. Use conceits, analogies, and sensitive language to produce a further immersive experience.

8. Structured Formatting

Break down your content into fluently digestible sections with headlines, heads, and pellet points. A well- organized structure makes it easier for compendiums to navigate and grasp the crucial points.

9. Engage feelings

Emotional resonance is a important tool in witching content. Appeal to compendiums ' feelings by telling relatable stories, using compassionate language, and addressing their pain points.

10. Incorporate Data and Research

Back up your points with believable data, exploration, and statistics. This not only adds credibility to your content but also shows that you've done your schoolwork.

11. Use Conversational Tone

Write as if you are having a discussion with your compendiums . Avoid exorbitantly formal language and slang that might part your followership.

12. Surprise and Curiosity

Incorporate surprising data, unanticipated angles, or counterintuitive perceptivity to keep compendiums intrigued and curious to learn further.

13.Call to Action(CTA)

Encourage anthology engagement with a clear and compelling call to action. Whether it's opining, participating, subscribing, or taking a specific action, guide your compendiums on what to do next.

14. Variety in Content Types

Trial with different types of content similar as how- to attendants, listicles, case studies, interviews, and opinion pieces. Variety keeps your content fresh and caters to different anthology preferences.

15. Edit and Polish

Noway underrate the power of thorough editing. exclude grammatical crimes, ameliorate judgment structure, and insure your content flows seamlessly.

16. Length and Readability

Pay attention to the length of your content. While long-form content can give in- depth perceptivity, make sure it's easy to read and skimmable.

17. Feedback and replication

Be open to feedback from your followership. dissect which content resonates the most and upgrade your approach grounded on what works. witching content requires a balance of creativity, understanding your followership, and employing colorful strategies to keep compendiums engaged. By casting compelling captions, incorporating liar, appealing to feelings, and furnishing value, you can produce content that captivates and leaves a lasting print on your followership. Flash back, practice and trial will help you upgrade your chops and find the perfect formula for witching content.

Creating Content with Value and Relevance

Creating content with value and relevance is a pivotal aspect of modern communication that caters to the ever-evolving demands of audiences. In a digital landscape saturated with an overwhelming influx of information, crafting content that stands out, engages, and resonates has become both an art and a science. This practice is not only confined to professional content creators and marketers but extends to individuals, businesses, and organizations seeking to establish meaningful connections with their target demographics.

At its core, content with value and relevance speaks directly to the needs, interests, and aspirations of its intended recipients. It transcends mere data and transforms into a dynamic tool for establishing rapport, trust, and authority. One of the primary tenets of value-laden content is offering insights, knowledge, or solutions that address a specific problem or question. This approach shifts content from being a mere promotional tool to becoming a resourceful asset that genuinely aids its consumers.

The creation of such content is underpinned by a deep understanding of the target audience. Researching their preferences, pain points, and behaviors is essential to tailor the content to their specific requirements. This empathetic approach ensures that the content is not only informative but also relatable, capturing the audience's attention and fostering a sense of connection.

Relevance is the key companion of value. Content must be timely, current, and pertinent to the prevailing trends and interests within the chosen niche or industry. Staying attuned to the pulse of the audience and the market enables content creators to produce pieces that strike a chord and remain in sync with the evolving discourse. Whether it's addressing recent developments, commenting on industry shifts, or predicting future trends, relevant content demonstrates a keen awareness of the world in which it operates.

Creating content with value and relevance is also closely tied to establishing authority and credibility. Consistently delivering accurate, well-researched, and insightful content positions the creator as a reliable source of information. This reputation is a potent asset in a landscape where misinformation and superficiality abound. An informed audience is more likely to engage, share, and return for more content, fostering a virtuous cycle of growth and influence.

A multi-faceted approach to content creation is essential to cater to diverse learning preferences and consumption habits. The use of various formats such as articles, videos, infographics, podcasts, and interactive content ensures that the message is effectively communicated across different channels and platforms. Additionally, incorporating storytelling elements into the content humanizes the message, making it relatable and memorable.

Search engine optimization (SEO) plays a pivotal role in the visibility of content. Value and relevance extend beyond human audiences; they also need to resonate with algorithms that rank and display content. Strategic use of keywords, meta tags, and structuring ensures that the content reaches its intended recipients through organic search results. This symbiotic relationship between content quality and SEO underscores the need for a balanced approach that caters to both humans and machines.

Engagement is the litmus test of content effectiveness. The value proposition should be clear from the outset, capturing attention and encouraging readers or viewers to delve deeper. Interactive elements, such as calls to action, polls, and comment sections, facilitate conversations and feedback, turning the content into a dynamic exchange rather than a monologue. Such engagement not only fosters community but also informs creators about the impact and reception of their content.

Evolution is the hallmark of successful content creation. Analyzing metrics such as views, shares, likes, and comments provides insights into the effectiveness of different strategies and topics. A data-driven approach empowers creators to refine their content over time, adapting to changing audience preferences and emerging trends. Flexibility and a willingness to innovate are crucial to maintaining relevance and staying ahead in the fast-paced digital arena.

Creating content with value and relevance is an intricate dance between understanding the audience, delivering timely insights, and maintaining credibility. It's a fusion of empathy and strategy, requiring constant adaptation and refinement. By addressing the specific needs of the audience, staying current, and fostering engagement, content creators can forge meaningful connections, establish authority, and navigate the intricate landscape of modern communication. In an age where attention is a scarce commodity, offering content that enriches, informs, and resonates is an invaluable skill that transcends industries and empowers effective communication.

CHAPTER 6
Channels and Distribution

Channels and distribution are pivotal components of any business strategy, determining how products and services reach consumers. An effective channel strategy ensures that goods flow seamlessly from manufacturers to end-users, optimizing accessibility and value creation. This intricate web of interactions involves various intermediaries, strategies, and considerations, ultimately shaping the success and competitiveness of a company.

Distribution channels encompass the routes through which products travel, connecting producers with consumers. They can be direct or indirect, involving varying levels of intermediaries. Direct channels involve the manufacturer selling directly to the consumer, bypassing intermediaries. Indirect channels, on the other hand, utilize intermediaries like wholesalers, retailers, and agents. Each channel type has its advantages and disadvantages, and the choice depends on factors such as product nature, target market, and company resources.

Wholesalers play a significant role in distribution, buying large quantities from manufacturers and selling smaller quantities to retailers. They provide economies of scale, storage facilities, and reduced logistical complexities for manufacturers. Retailers, in turn, offer a physical or online presence for consumers to access products conveniently. Their role extends beyond sales to providing information, after-sales service, and enhancing the overall customer experience.

E-commerce has revolutionized distribution channels, introducing new paradigms. The direct-to-consumer (DTC) model, employed by companies like Warby Parker and Casper, leverages online platforms to eliminate intermediaries and establish a direct link with customers. This fosters brand loyalty, permits better customer insights, and offers higher profit margins. Conversely, the marketplace model, as seen on Amazon and eBay, brings numerous sellers onto one platform, offering consumers unparalleled product variety and convenience.

The choice of distribution channel profoundly influences a company's competitive edge. Factors like market coverage, control, and cost considerations come into play. Intensive distribution seeks to saturate the market with the product, ideal for low-cost, high-frequency items like snacks. Selective distribution involves a limited number of outlets, maintaining a balance between market coverage and control, often seen in consumer electronics. Exclusive distribution, observed in luxury brands, involves a single outlet in a large area, enhancing exclusivity and brand image.

Distribution channels are not static; they adapt to market trends and consumer behaviors. Omni-channel distribution recognizes that customers interact with a brand through various touchpoints: physical stores, websites, mobile apps, and social media. This approach demands seamless integration, ensuring a consistent experience regardless of the channel chosen. Such integration requires sophisticated inventory management and real-time communication to avoid issues like stockouts or conflicting pricing.

The geographic scope of distribution channels adds another layer of complexity. Globalization has enabled companies to access international markets, necessitating intricate networks of importers, distributors, and retailers. The choice between standardized and localized distribution plays a crucial role. Standardization employs uniform distribution strategies across countries, reaping economies of scale, but may neglect local preferences. Localization tailors distribution to each market's unique characteristics, accommodating cultural, legal, and infrastructural variations.

Efficient distribution hinges on robust logistical and supply chain management. Timely and accurate order processing, inventory management, transportation, and warehousing are vital. Technology, such as warehouse management systems and transport optimization software, has streamlined these processes. Just-in-time (JIT) and vendor-managed inventory (VMI) systems reduce holding costs by synchronizing production and distribution, while third-party logistics (3PL) providers offer specialized expertise and resources.

The evolving landscape of distribution channels calls for continuous analysis and adaptation. Market research and consumer insights guide strategic decisions, helping companies anticipate changing demands and preferences. Evaluating channel performance involves metrics like sales volume, inventory turnover, and customer satisfaction. Feedback loops, both from consumers and intermediaries, facilitate improvements and address bottlenecks.

Distribution channels are the arteries of commerce, facilitating the movement of goods from producers to consumers. The choice of distribution strategy impacts market accessibility, customer experience, and a company's bottom line. The dynamic interplay of direct and indirect channels, supported by technological advancements, reshapes traditional paradigms.

Exploring Multichannel Marketing

In today's fast-paced digital landscape, businesses are constantly seeking innovative ways to reach and engage with their target audiences. Multichannel marketing has emerged as a powerful strategy that allows companies to connect with customers through multiple platforms and touchpoints. This approach acknowledges the diverse ways individuals consume information and make purchasing decisions, ensuring a brand's presence across various channels. This essay delves into the concept of multichannel marketing, its benefits, challenges, and best practices, highlighting its significance in enhancing customer experiences and driving business growth.

Multichannel marketing involves leveraging a mix of online and offline channels to communicate with customers. These channels include social media, email, websites, physical stores, mobile apps, direct mail, and more. Unlike traditional single-channel approaches, multichannel marketing recognizes that consumers interact with brands on their terms, choosing the channels that suit their preferences and needs. By establishing a consistent and coordinated presence across these channels, companies can effectively reach a wider audience and foster deeper connections.

One of the key benefits of multichannel marketing is its ability to enhance customer experiences. By providing a seamless transition between channels, businesses create a cohesive brand identity that resonates with consumers. A customer who discovers a product on social media should find the same product and messaging on the website or in a physical store. This continuity instills trust and credibility, as customers perceive the brand as attentive to their preferences and consistent in its messaging.

Moreover, multichannel marketing can significantly impact sales and conversions. Studies indicate that customers who engage with a brand through multiple channels tend to spend more than those who only interact through a single channel. This is known as the "omnichannel premium." By facilitating a more comprehensive customer journey, multichannel marketing increases the likelihood of conversions and repeat purchases. For instance, a customer might first encounter a product on social media, research it on the website, visit a physical store to see it in person, and finally make the purchase online. Each touchpoint contributes to the overall decision-making process.

However, implementing a successful multichannel marketing strategy is not without its challenges. Coordinating messaging and branding across various channels can be complex, requiring careful planning and execution. Inconsistencies in messaging or design can confuse customers and dilute the brand's impact. Additionally, the abundance of channels available can make it difficult to determine which ones are most effective for a particular business. Allocating resources to each channel without a clear strategy can result in inefficiencies and wasted investments.

To overcome these challenges, businesses must adopt best practices for multichannel marketing. First and foremost, understanding the target audience is essential. By knowing where their customers are most active and receptive, companies can prioritize channels that align with customer preferences. Conducting thorough market research and leveraging data analytics can provide valuable insights into consumer behavior and channel performance.

Secondly, maintaining consistency is paramount. Brands should establish clear guidelines for messaging, tone, and visual identity to ensure a unified presence across channels. This not only reinforces brand recognition but also helps build trust and credibility.

Furthermore, businesses should embrace technology that enables seamless integration and automation. Marketing automation platforms can streamline the process of managing multiple channels, ensuring that messages are delivered at the right time and to the right audience. Personalization is also crucial—tailoring content to suit the preferences and behaviors of individual customers enhances engagement and encourages interaction.

Multichannel marketing has evolved into an indispensable strategy for modern businesses. Its ability to create cohesive customer experiences, boost sales, and foster brand loyalty makes it a compelling approach in an increasingly interconnected world. While challenges such as maintaining consistency and determining effective channels exist, these can be overcome through diligent planning, data-driven insights, and technological integration. As consumer behavior continues to evolve, companies that prioritize multichannel marketing are better positioned to thrive in a competitive marketplace. By embracing the diversity of channels available, businesses can build lasting relationships with their customers and drive sustainable growth.

Selecting the Right Channels for Your Business

In the dynamic geography of moment's business world, opting the right channels to reach your target followership is of consummate significance. With an array of communication platforms and mediums available, businesses must make strategic choices to effectively engage their guests and drive growth. The process of channel selection involves understanding your followership, assessing colorful options, and aligning your brand communication with the most suitable platforms. This composition explores the critical considerations and way involved in opting the right channels for your business. Understanding Your followership The foundation of effective channel selection lies in a comprehensive understanding of your target followership. Without a clear grasp of their preferences, habits, and demographics, any channel choice becomes a shot in the dark. Conducting thorough request exploration, checks, and assaying client data are essential way to develop buyer personas. These personas represent typical guests and guide your opinions by revealing where they spend their time, how they consume content, and what resonates with them. assessing Channel Options Once followership perceptivity are gathered, it's time to estimate the plethora of channel options available. From traditional mediums like TV, radio, and print to digital platforms like social media, dispatch, and websites, each channel offers unique benefits and challenges. The felicity of a channel depends on factors similar as the nature of your product or service, your brand's voice, and your coffers.

1. Social Media In the digital age, social media channels like Facebook, Instagram, Twitter, LinkedIn, and TikTok have come integral for business communication. They offer targeted advertising, real-time engagement, and the capability to showcase your brand's personality. Choosing the right platform depends on your followership demographics – LinkedIn for B2B relations, Instagram for visual content, and TikTok for a youngish demographic.

2. Content Marketing Blogs, vids, podcasts, and other forms of content marketing can establish your authority and give value to your followership. Platforms like YouTube and Medium are ideal for participating in-depth content, while podcasts can tap into cult on platforms like Spotify and Apple Podcasts.

3. Dispatch Marketing Dispatch remains a important tool for reaching a more engaged followership. It's particular, direct, and allows for targeted communication. erecting a subscriber list and casting compelling dispatch juggernauts can nurture leads and retain guests.

4. Traditional Media Despite the digital shift, traditional media still holds its ground. Depending on your target followership, radio, TV, and print media might be effective, especially for original businesses or diligence with a mature demographic.

5. Influencer Collaborations Influencer marketing leverages the fashionability of individualities on platforms like Instagram and YouTube to promote your products. uniting with the right influencers can help you tap into their follower base and gain credibility.

6. Donated Advertising Online advertising through platforms like Google Advertisements and Facebook Advertisements can deliver targeted dispatches to specific parts of your followership. This is especially effective when combined with data- driven perceptivity from your followership exploration.

7. Direct Outreach Personalized outreach, similar as phone calls or direct dispatches, can establish a more direct connection with implicit guests. This approach is frequently used in B2B deals but can also work in certain B2C scripts. Aligning with Brand Communication thickness across channels is crucial to erecting a strong brand image. Your brand's voice, values, and communication should remain harmonious anyhow of the channel chosen. Whether it's a facetious tweet or a study- provoking blog post, the substance of your brand should shine through. Testing and Measuring The dynamic nature of consumer preferences and request trends demands an nimble approach. After channel selection, it's pivotal to continuously test and measure the effectiveness of your chosen channels. This can be done through analytics tools, tracking engagement criteria , conversion rates, and client feedback.

Regularly conforming your strategies grounded on these perceptivity ensures you stay aligned with your followership's preferences. opting the right channels for your business is a multifaceted bid that requires a deep understanding of your followership, strategic evaluation of options, and alignment with your brand's identity. The digital age offers an array of channels, each with its own strengths, but the key lies in choosing those that reverberate most with your target followership. Through harmonious messaging, thorough testing, and a amenability to acclimatize, businesses can produce a potent channel strategy that drives engagement, growth, and lasting client connections.

CHAPTER 7
Data-Driven Decision Making

In the digital age, where information flows at an unprecedented rate, businesses have access to an enormous amount of data. This data, if leveraged effectively, can revolutionize the way decisions are made across various domains, including marketing. Data-driven decision making in marketing is a strategic approach that involves using data analytics and insights to guide marketing strategies, campaigns, and initiatives. This methodology has become increasingly essential for businesses seeking to enhance their understanding of consumer behavior, optimize resource allocation, and ultimately achieve better outcomes.

At the heart of data-driven decision making lies the process of collecting, analyzing, and interpreting data. This process is not limited to the quantitative metrics associated with traditional marketing campaigns but extends to the more intricate details of customer interactions, preferences, and sentiments. By tapping into a diverse array of data sources, such as website analytics, social media engagement, customer surveys, and sales figures, businesses can gain a holistic understanding of their target audience.

The foundation of data-driven marketing is rooted in segmentation and targeting. Data analytics allow marketers to divide their audience into distinct segments based on characteristics such as demographics, psychographics, and behavior. These segments can then be targeted with personalized messages and offerings, increasing the relevance and effectiveness of marketing efforts. For instance, an e-commerce platform can use past purchase data to recommend products that align with a customer's preferences, thereby enhancing the likelihood of conversion.

Furthermore, data-driven decision making empowers marketers to track and measure the performance of their campaigns in real time. This agility enables rapid adjustments based on emerging trends and consumer responses. If a particular campaign is not yielding the desired results, marketers can pivot swiftly, reallocating resources to more promising strategies. This iterative process of testing, analyzing, and optimizing is known as A/B testing. It allows marketers to make informed decisions by comparing the performance of two variations of a marketing element, such as an email subject line or a website layout.

Personalization is a cornerstone of modern marketing, and data-driven approaches take personalization to new heights. By delving into customer data, businesses can understand individual preferences and tailor marketing messages that resonate on a personal level. This not only enhances customer engagement but also fosters brand loyalty. For instance, streaming platforms use viewing history and genre preferences to curate content recommendations, providing users with a unique and enjoyable experience.

In addition to enhancing customer experiences, data-driven marketing strategies also optimize resource allocation. Limited marketing budgets require careful planning to maximize return on investment (ROI). By analyzing historical data and performance metrics, businesses can identify which channels and campaigns generate the highest ROI. This insight empowers them to allocate resources effectively, focusing on strategies that yield the best results. For instance, if data reveals that a significant portion of a target audience engages with the brand on social media, reallocating resources from less effective channels to social media campaigns can yield higher returns.

The marriage of data and marketing also extends to predictive analytics, where historical data is used to forecast future trends and behaviors. This enables businesses to anticipate market shifts and tailor their strategies accordingly. Predictive analytics can help identify potential high-value customers, enabling businesses to proactively engage with them. For instance, a telecommunications company might use predictive analytics to identify customers who are likely to churn and offer them personalized incentives to retain their loyalty.

However, data-driven decision making in marketing is not without its challenges. The sheer volume of data available can be overwhelming, making it crucial for businesses to invest in robust data management and analysis tools. Privacy concerns also come to the forefront, necessitating compliance with data protection regulations and ensuring transparent data usage policies. Moreover, the human element remains vital in interpreting data accurately and translating insights into actionable strategies.

Data-driven decision making has reshaped the landscape of marketing. By harnessing the power of data analytics, businesses can gain profound insights into consumer behavior, preferences, and trends. This understanding enables the creation of highly targeted and personalized marketing campaigns that resonate with audiences on a personal level.

Harnessing the Insights of Marketing Analytics

In moment's fleetly evolving business geography, the part of marketing has transcended its traditional boundaries. It has converted into a data- driven discipline, with marketing analytics at its core. This paradigm shift stems from the exponential growth of digital platforms, which has generated an immense volume of data. To navigate this data-rich terrain successfully, businesses are turning to marketing analytics to prize precious perceptivity. This essay delves into the mechanisms of how employing these perceptivity through marketing analytics works, expounding its stages, methodologies, and the impact it holds. Marketing analytics is the methodical process of collecting, measuring, assaying, and interpreting data related to marketing sweats. It aims to disinter patterns, trends, correlations, and perceptivity that can drive informed decision- timber. This process is sustained by a multifaceted frame that encompasses colorful stages, each contributing to the overall effectiveness of marketing strategies.

Data Collection and Aggregation

The foundation of marketing analytics lies in data collection. Enterprises accumulate vast quantities of data from different sources, including social media, client relations, website business, and deals records. This raw data is also added up and consolidated in data depositories. This step is pivotal as the delicacy and comprehensiveness of data impact the quality of perceptivity generated.

Data Cleaning and Preparation

Raw data is frequently unshaped, inconsistent, and replete with crimes. The data cleaning and medication phase involve enriching the collected data, barring duplicates, correcting inaccuracies, and transubstantiating data into a standardized format. This standardized dataset serves as the base for posterior analysis, icing that the perceptivity drawn are dependable and meaningful.

Exploratory Data Analysis(EDA)

EDA involves the original examination of data through summary statistics, visualizations, and primary perceptivity. This step helps judges gain a primary understanding of the data, identify trends, and formulate suppositions for farther disquisition. EDA acts as a compass, guiding judges towards the areas with the most implicit for precious perceptivity.

operation of Analytical Models

The heart of marketing analytics lies in the operation of logical models. These models range from introductory statistical styles to advanced machine learning algorithms. They check the data to uncover retired patterns, correlations, and prophetic perceptivity. For case, client segmentation models can classify guests into distinct groups grounded on actions, abetting in targeted marketing sweats.

Prophetic Analytics

Prophetic analytics utilizes literal data to read unborn trends and issues. By relating patterns and connections within the data, prophetic models can anticipate client geste , request oscillations, and the impact of colorful marketing strategies. This enables businesses to proactively acclimatize their approaches, enhancing their competitiveness.

Descriptive Analytics

Descriptive analytics focuses on recapitulating literal data to give a comprehensive shot of once performance. crucial performance pointers(KPIs) are frequently used to measure the success of marketing juggernauts, product launches, and overall business pretensions. Descriptive analytics aids in assessing what has happed and provides perceptivity into the effectiveness of once strategies.

Conventional Analytics

Conventional analytics takes perceptivity a step further by not only revealing what has happed and why but also suggesting optimal conduct for asked issues. This involves script analysis and simulation to recommend the stylish course of action. For case, conventional analytics can guide marketers on the ideal allocation of coffers across colorful marketing channels to maximize ROI.

Data Visualization and Reporting

The perceptivity deduced from marketing analytics are frequently communicated through data visualization and reporting tools. Visualizations similar as maps, graphs, and dashboards help stakeholders comprehend complex perceptivity snappily and make informed opinions. Effective data visualization transforms raw figures into practicable perceptivity, bridging the gap between judges and decision- makers.

Iterative Process and nonstop enhancement

employing marketing perceptivity through analytics isn't a one- time bid; it's a nonstop process. As the request geography evolves and new data aqueducts crop , marketers need to continuously upgrade their approaches. This involves an iterative cycle of data collection, analysis, strategy perpetration, and performance evaluation. perceptivity gained from once juggernauts inform unborn trials, leading to a cycle of nonstop enhancement. Impact and unborn Counteraccusations The impact of employing marketing analytics perceptivity is profound. Businesses can optimize marketing spend, knitter juggernauts to specific client parts, enhance client gests , and make strategic opinions backed by data. By aligning marketing strategies with client preferences and request trends, associations can achieve advanced ROI and foster client fidelity. Looking ahead, the elaboration of marketing analytics is poised to continue. With advancements in artificial intelligence and machine literacy, prophetic and conventional analytics will come more sophisticated. The integration of real- time data and the Internet of effects(IoT) will offer indeed deeper perceptivity into consumer gest and preferences. In the ultramodern business geography, the art of marketing is thick from the wisdom of analytics. employing marketing perceptivity through analytics involves a methodical process that encompasses data collection, cleaning, analysis, and interpretation. This process empowers businesses to make informed opinions, optimize strategies, and stay ahead in a competitive terrain. As technology continues to advance, the perceptivity picked from marketing analytics will remain vital in driving success and invention.

CHAPTER 8
Integrating the Mastery Code

In moment's presto- paced and dynamic business geography, effective marketing strategies are the linchpin for success. The conventional marketing approaches have evolved into a realm where personalization, robotization, and data- driven opinions control supreme. Among these innovative strategies, the conception of the" Mastery Code Marketing" emerges as a important tool to unleash exponential growth and competitive advantage. This essay explores the substance of Mastery Code Marketing, its crucial factors, and the unequaled benefits it brings to ultramodern businesses. Mastery Code Marketing represents a paradigm shift from traditional marketing methodologies. It encapsulates a comprehensive frame that leverages substantiated content, advanced analytics, and strategic community to produce a holistic marketing approach. The core gospel of this approach centers around understanding the complications of client geste, conforming marketing sweats in real-time, and fostering long- term connections through authentic engagement. By integrating Mastery Code Marketing, businesses can align their strategies with the dynamic request palpitation, icing advanced applicability and resonance among their target followership. At the heart of Mastery Code Marketing lies the mastery of data. In the digital age, information is a precious currency. The vacuity of vast quantities of consumer data empowers marketers to ripen perceptivity into preferences, purchase patterns, and pain points. By employing the eventuality of data analytics, businesses can draft largely individualized juggernauts that connect with individualities on a deeper position. Mastery Code Marketing enables the creation of acclimatized content, curated offers, and precisely timed relations, fostering a sense of exclusivity and affinity. Central to this approach is the conception of strategic community. Mastery Code Marketing encourages the confluence of colorful marketing channels, both online and offline, to produce a cohesive brand experience. Whether it's through social media, dispatch marketing, influencer hookups, or immersive in- person events, the end is to produce a flawless narrative that resonates with guests. This integration not only enhances brand recall but also nurtures a sense of belonging and community among consumers. likewise, the Mastery Code Marketing approach thrives on dexterity and rigidity. The traditional static marketing plans are replaced by dynamic strategies that respond to real- time feedback and request shifts. using technologies similar as artificial intelligence and machine literacy, businesses can optimize their juggernauts on the cover. This adaptiveness ensures that coffers are allocated efficiently, and the marketing dispatches remain applicable and compelling in an ever- changing geography. One of the crucial advantages of Mastery Code Marketing is its measurable impact. Unlike traditional strategies where gauging success can be fugitive, this approach provides robust analytics and performance criteria . Businesses can track engagement rates, conversion rates, client trip progression, and much further. These perceptivity enable data- driven decision- timber, allowing for nonstop refinement and enhancement of marketing sweats. Mastery Code Marketing turns the guessing game of marketing into a precise wisdom. Integrating this approach also enhances client fidelity and advocacy. By creating individualized gests and addressing individual requirements, businesses foster a sense of attachment and fidelity among their guests. Satisfied guests are more likely to come brand lawyers, spreading positive word- of- mouth and amplifying the brand's reach organically. This righteous cycle contributes to sustainable growth and a strong competitive edge. still, the relinquishment of Mastery Code Marketing comes with its challenges. perpetration requires a deep understanding of data sequestration and ethical considerations. The collection and application of client data must align with nonsupervisory guidelines and respect individual sequestration rights. also, integrating multiple marketing channels necessitates flawless collaboration and resource allocation, which can be complex to achieve. Mastery Code Marketing represents a groundbreaking approach to contemporary marketing strategies. By using data mastery, strategic community, and real- time rigidity, businesses can produce a potent formula for success in a fast- evolving digital geography. The benefits of substantiated engagement, measurable impact, and enhanced client fidelity make this approach an necessary tool for ultramodern businesses aiming to thrive in a competitive terrain. As technology continues to evolve and consumer prospects evolve with it, the integration of the Mastery Code Marketing approach will probably come not just a choice, but a necessity for sustained growth and applicability.

Case Studies of Successful Marketing Mastery Implementation

I'd be happy to provide you with a few brief case studies of successful marketing mastery implementations. Each of these examples showcases how effective marketing strategies and tactics can lead to impressive outcomes for businesses.

1. Apple's Product Launches: Creating Anticipation

Apple has consistently demonstrated exceptional marketing mastery with its product launches. The company builds anticipation by teasing new features and design elements, keeping information limited until the launch event. This strategy generates excitement and curiosity among consumers, encouraging them to tune in and learn about the latest offerings. The "one more thing" surprise element has become iconic, fueling intense media coverage and consumer discussions.

2. Dollar Shave Club: Disruptive Content Marketing

Dollar Shave Club disrupted the grooming industry by adopting a bold and humorous content marketing approach. Their launch video, featuring the CEO's charismatic pitch, quickly went viral. By addressing common frustrations with traditional razor brands and presenting their subscription model in a fun and engaging way, the company garnered millions of views, leading to a massive increase in subscribers practically overnight.

3. Nike's "Just Do It" Campaign Empowering Messaging

Nike's "Just Do It" campaign is a textbook example of powerful messaging. By focusing on the aspirational aspects of sports and fitness, Nike connected with consumers on an emotional level, inspiring them to push their limits and achieve greatness. This campaign not only solidified Nike's position as a leading athletic brand but also created a lasting cultural catchphrase.

4. Coca-Cola's Personalization Share a Coke Campaign

Coca-Cola's "Share a Coke" campaign personalized its packaging by replacing the brand's logo with popular names. This simple yet impactful idea led to a surge in social media engagement as people sought out bottles with their names on them and shared photos online. The campaign effectively reinforced a sense of personal connection with the brand, resulting in increased sales and consumer engagement.

5. Red Bull's Extreme Marketing Stunts Creating Brand Lifestyle

Red Bull has mastered the art of experiential marketing by sponsoring extreme sports events and stunts. By aligning with adrenaline-fueled activities, the brand effectively associates itself with an adventurous and high-energy lifestyle. The most notable example is Felix Baumgartner's record-breaking space jump, which not only captured the world's attention but also solidified Red Bull's image as a daring and innovative brand.

6. Airbnb's User-Generated Content: Building Trust

Airbnb's success is partly attributed to its user-generated content strategy. By allowing hosts to share photos and stories of their properties and experiences, Airbnb built a sense of trust and authenticity. Prospective travelers could visualize their stays and feel more confident in their bookings. This strategy helped Airbnb rapidly grow its user base and establish itself as a trusted platform for accommodations.

7. Old Spice's Rebranding Appeal to New Demographics

Old Spice successfully reinvented itself by rebranding to appeal to a younger demographic. Through clever and humorous advertising campaigns, the brand shed its outdated image and positioned itself as edgy and relevant. The "The Man Your Man Could Smell Like" campaign, featuring Isaiah Mustafa, went viral, revitalizing the brand and increasing sales substantially.

These case studies highlight the importance of innovative marketing strategies and the impact they can have on a company's success. Whether through viral content, personalized experiences, emotional messaging, or aligning with aspirational lifestyles, these brands leveraged marketing mastery to capture consumer attention, build trust, and drive remarkable business growth.

Navigating Technological Disruptions in Marketing

In an era defined by rapid technological advancement, the marketing landscape is undergoing profound transformations. The convergence of digital innovation, data analytics, and consumer behavior has led to a paradigm shift in how businesses connect with their target audiences. Navigating these technological disruptions has become a pivotal challenge for marketers worldwide. This essay explores the key dimensions of this challenge, the strategies employed to address it, and the potential implications for the future of marketing.

The advent of digital technology has revolutionized how brands engage with consumers. The proliferation of smartphones, social media platforms, and online shopping has reshaped the way people discover, interact with, and purchase products. As a result, marketing strategies have evolved from traditional mass advertising to personalized, data-driven approaches. The rise of social media influencers, content marketing, and search engine optimization reflects this shift, as companies strive to create relevant and engaging experiences that resonate with individual preferences.

Data, often referred to as the "new oil," has become the cornerstone of modern marketing. Technological disruptions have enabled the collection, analysis, and utilization of vast amounts of consumer data. Marketers can now decipher intricate patterns of behavior, preferences, and purchasing habits. This insight empowers them to tailor campaigns with pinpoint accuracy, enhancing the likelihood of resonating with the target audience. However, this data-driven approach also raises ethical concerns about consumer privacy and the responsible use of personal information.

Artificial Intelligence (AI) and machine learning are driving remarkable changes in marketing strategies. These technologies enable predictive analytics, allowing marketers to forecast future trends based on historical data. Chatbots and virtual assistants provide instant customer support, enhancing user experiences and driving customer satisfaction. AI-driven content generation streamlines the creative process, producing targeted messages and advertisements. Yet, the extent to which AI should replace human creativity and decision-making remains a subject of debate.

E-commerce has experienced explosive growth, reshaping retail and challenging traditional marketing channels. The convenience of online shopping, coupled with personalized recommendations, has reshaped consumer expectations. Consequently, brick-and-mortar stores face pressure to adapt, blending physical experiences with digital elements to create a seamless omnichannel journey. This integration requires marketers to orchestrate consistent messaging and branding across various touchpoints, ensuring a cohesive and immersive customer experience.

Social media platforms have become ubiquitous, offering marketers unprecedented access to global audiences. The viral nature of social content can lead to rapid brand exposure, but it also demands agility and responsiveness. Negative feedback or a social media crisis can spread quickly, underscoring the need for robust reputation management strategies. Authenticity has emerged as a core value, with consumers favoring brands that demonstrate genuine social responsibility and engage in meaningful dialogues.

Agility is a cornerstone of successful marketing amidst technological disruptions. The pace of innovation requires marketers to be adaptable, ready to embrace emerging platforms and technologies. Traditional long-term campaigns are being replaced by iterative, data-informed approaches that can be adjusted on the fly. A/B testing, for instance, allows marketers to compare different versions of content and refine strategies based on real-time performance data. This iterative approach minimizes risks and maximizes the impact of marketing efforts.

Collaboration between marketing and IT departments is imperative in navigating technological disruptions. Marketing teams need IT expertise to implement and manage complex data analytics tools, customer relationship management (CRM) systems, and marketing automation platforms. Conversely, IT professionals require a deep understanding of marketing principles to effectively translate business objectives into technological solutions. This interdisciplinary partnership ensures that technological implementations align with marketing goals, fostering innovation and efficiency.

The future of marketing in the face of technological disruptions presents a mixture of opportunities and challenges. The continued advancement of AI and machine learning will likely refine consumer insights, enabling even more precise targeting. However, the ethical use of AI, data privacy regulations, and potential consumer backlash against invasive practices could reshape the boundaries of marketing strategies. Striking the right balance between personalization and privacy will be paramount.

Navigating technological disruptions in marketing necessitates a multifaceted approach. It requires a keen understanding of digital innovation, data analytics, and evolving consumer behaviors. Successful marketers embrace data-driven decision-making, harness the power of AI, and maintain an agile stance to adapt to changing trends. Collaboration between IT and marketing departments, along with a commitment to ethical practices, will define the effectiveness of marketing efforts. As technology continues to reshape the marketing landscape, the ability to harness its power while upholding consumer trust will determine the industry's trajectory.

CHAPTER 9

Beyond Mastery: Innovations and Trends

In a rapidly evolving world, the pursuit of mastery has taken on new dimensions. Once limited to the realms of art, music, and craftsmanship, the concept of mastery now extends far beyond these traditional domains. In today's landscape, mastery encapsulates the ability to navigate complex innovations and embrace emerging trends across various fields. The interplay between mastery, innovation, and trends has become a dynamic force shaping industries, societies, and individuals.

Mastery, traditionally associated with achieving the highest level of proficiency in a particular skill or discipline, has seen a shift in its definition. While technical prowess remains essential, the definition of mastery has expanded to include adaptability, creativity, and a proactive approach to change. The master of today not only excels in their chosen field but also possesses the agility to learn and apply new skills rapidly. This shift can be attributed to the rapid pace of innovation, which has disrupted established norms and necessitated a continuous cycle of learning.

Innovation, the catalyst for this paradigm shift, plays a central role in propelling mastery beyond its conventional boundaries. The 21st century is characterized by unprecedented technological advancements and groundbreaking ideas that constantly challenge the status quo. Innovations such as artificial intelligence, biotechnology, renewable energy solutions, and the digitalization of industries are revolutionizing the way we live and work. The modern master leverages these innovations to amplify their impact, harnessing technology as a tool to reach new heights of achievement.

However, the relationship between mastery and innovation is not unidirectional. Mastery itself has become a driving force behind innovation. Experts who have attained mastery in their domains often identify gaps or inefficiencies that others might overlook. This keen understanding allows them to innovate solutions that address real-world problems more effectively. For instance, Elon Musk's mastery in both engineering and business has led to innovations like SpaceX and Tesla, reshaping space travel and transportation.

Yet, mastery and innovation alone are insufficient in today's context. The third crucial component is the identification and incorporation of emerging trends. Trends are the manifestations of societal shifts, consumer behaviors, and market demands. A true master recognizes these trends and adapts their strategies accordingly. Whether it's the growing demand for sustainable products, the rise of the gig economy, or the increased focus on mental health, incorporating these trends into one's mastery ensures continued relevance and influence.

The intersection of mastery, innovation, and trends is particularly evident in business. Organizations that prioritize mastery cultivate a workforce equipped with the skills needed to drive innovation. These organizations not only adapt to change but also initiate it, setting industry standards. Take Apple, for example; their commitment to design mastery, innovative thinking, and anticipation of consumer trends has propelled them to the forefront of the technology sector.

Education, too, is undergoing a transformation due to this synergy. The traditional model of education emphasized the acquisition of knowledge, but modern education emphasizes the development of critical thinking, problem-solving, and adaptability - qualities synonymous with mastery. Educators now prepare students to embrace innovation and stay attuned to trends that will shape their future careers.

The concept of mastery has transcended its historical boundaries, becoming a multifaceted amalgamation of proficiency, innovation, and trend adaptation. The modern master is an agile learner, leveraging innovation to propel their craft and incorporating emerging trends to maintain relevance. Mastery is no longer an endpoint but a dynamic journey of growth. As the world continues to evolve, the interplay between mastery, innovation, and trends will remain a potent force, shaping industries, societies, and the very nature of expertise itself.

AI and Automation in Marketing

In recent years, the landscape of marketing has undergone a profound transformation, largely fueled by the rapid advancements in artificial intelligence (AI) and automation technologies. This convergence has not only reshaped the way businesses connect with their audiences but has also ushered in a new era of efficiency, personalization, and data-driven decision-making. As AI continues to evolve and permeate various industries, its integration with marketing strategies has proven to be a game-changer, offering unprecedented opportunities and challenges.

One of the most significant contributions of AI and automation to marketing is the ability to process and analyze vast amounts of data at speeds and accuracies that were once unthinkable. Through machine learning algorithms, AI can sift through customer behaviors, preferences, and interactions to extract valuable insights. These insights, in turn, enable marketers to create highly targeted and personalized campaigns, maximizing the chances of engagement and conversion. This data-driven approach minimizes guesswork, allowing marketing efforts to be focused on what truly resonates with the audience.

Automation has taken over repetitive and time-consuming tasks, liberating marketers to concentrate on more creative and strategic aspects of their roles. Email marketing, for instance, has been revolutionized by AI-powered tools that can segment audiences, craft customized messages, and optimize delivery times for maximum impact. Social media scheduling and posting, once a manual chore, are now seamlessly managed by automation platforms, ensuring a consistent online presence without constant manual intervention.

The rise of chatbots and virtual assistants showcases AI's pivotal role in enhancing customer experiences. These intelligent systems can engage with customers in real time, answering queries, providing product recommendations, and even facilitating purchases. This 24/7 availability not only boosts customer satisfaction but also frees up human resources that can be allocated to more complex tasks requiring emotional intelligence and creativity.

Personalization lies at the heart of effective marketing, and AI has elevated personalization to unprecedented heights. By analyzing customer data, AI can predict individual preferences and behaviors, enabling marketers to deliver tailor-made content and product suggestions. This level of personalization fosters a stronger sense of connection between the brand and the consumer, driving customer loyalty and repeat business.

However, as AI and automation reshape marketing practices, ethical considerations come to the forefront. Concerns about data privacy and security are amplified as AI relies heavily on personal information. Striking a balance between personalization and privacy becomes crucial to maintain consumer trust. Moreover, the fear of job displacement due to automation is not unfounded. While AI streamlines processes, human creativity, intuition, and empathy remain irreplaceable. Thus, a recalibration of the workforce is essential, with a focus on upskilling and reskilling to harness AI's potential rather than be threatened by it.

AI's predictive capabilities are a cornerstone of its marketing applications. By analyzing historical data and identifying patterns, AI can forecast market trends and consumer behavior. This invaluable insight allows businesses to stay ahead of the curve, making informed decisions about product development, inventory management, and campaign strategies. Predictive analytics empowers marketers to allocate resources more effectively and adapt strategies proactively, reducing risks and enhancing competitiveness.

Social media monitoring and sentiment analysis have also been revolutionized by AI. Brands can now gain real-time insights into how their products are being discussed online, allowing them to respond promptly to customer feedback and manage potential crises. AI's natural language processing capabilities enable sentiment analysis, which gauges public opinion about the brand, helping companies refine their messaging and engagement strategies.

In the realm of content creation, AI has demonstrated its potential to assist and augment human creativity. Automated tools can generate written content, design visuals, and even compose music. While AI-generated content is not without flaws and lacks the depth of human ingenuity, it can be a valuable asset in generating large volumes of content quickly, freeing marketers to focus on higher-order tasks.

AI and automation have reshaped the marketing landscape, offering unparalleled opportunities for efficiency, personalization, and data-driven decision-making. By analyzing vast amounts of data, automating repetitive tasks, and enhancing customer experiences, AI has become an indispensable tool for modern marketers.

Emerging Trends Shaping the Future of Marketing

In a world driven by constant technological advancements and evolving consumer behaviors, the landscape of marketing is undergoing a profound transformation. Traditional marketing strategies are being redefined and reshaped by a plethora of emerging trends that are revolutionizing how businesses engage with their target audiences. These trends are not only reshaping the future of marketing but also redefining the way companies approach branding, customer engagement, and business growth. In this essay, we will delve into some of the most prominent emerging trends that are shaping the future of marketing.

1. Personalization and Hyper-Targeting: One of the key trends shaping the future of marketing is the move towards hyper-personalization. With access to vast amounts of data, companies can now tailor their marketing messages and offerings to individual consumers based on their preferences, behaviors, and past interactions. This level of personalization creates a more meaningful and relevant connection between brands and consumers, enhancing customer engagement and loyalty.

2. Artificial Intelligence and Machine Learning: The integration of artificial intelligence (AI) and machine learning (ML) is another significant trend revolutionizing marketing. AI-powered tools analyze consumer data to predict trends, automate tasks, and optimize marketing campaigns. Chatbots and virtual assistants provide real-time customer support, while AI-driven algorithms refine ad targeting and content recommendations.

3. Content Marketing Evolution: Content remains king, but its form is evolving. Video content, live streaming, and interactive experiences are gaining prominence. Consumers are more likely to engage with dynamic and visually appealing content. This shift requires marketers to adapt their strategies to include multimedia elements that resonate with their target audience.

4. Influencer Marketing: Influencer marketing continues to grow as a powerful strategy. Collaborating with influencers allows brands to tap into their established audiences and build trust through genuine recommendations. Micro-influencers, with smaller but highly engaged followings, are also becoming more popular due to their authenticity and relatability.

5. Voice Search and Smart Speakers: The rise of voice-activated devices like smart speakers is changing how consumers search for information and make purchases. Optimizing content for voice search is becoming crucial, as the conversational nature of voice queries requires different keyword strategies and concise, direct answers.

6. Augmented Reality (AR) and Virtual Reality (VR): AR and VR technologies are transforming the way consumers experience products and services. Brands are leveraging these technologies to create immersive shopping experiences, allowing customers to "try before they buy" and visualize products in their real-world environments.

7. Data Privacy and Ethics: As data collection becomes more pervasive, concerns about data privacy and ethical use of consumer information are rising. Stricter regulations, such as the GDPR and CCPA, are forcing marketers to be more transparent about data collection practices and provide opt-in mechanisms.

8. Sustainability and Social Responsibility: Modern consumers are increasingly conscious of a brand's environmental and social impact. Companies that demonstrate a commitment to sustainability and social responsibility are gaining a competitive edge. Purpose-driven marketing that aligns with meaningful causes can resonate deeply with consumers.

9. 5G Technology: The rollout of 5G technology is set to revolutionize digital experiences. It will enable faster internet speeds, seamless streaming, and enhanced connectivity, paving the way for more interactive and real-time content delivery.

10. Ephemeral Content : Platforms like Instagram Stories and Snapchat have popularized ephemeral content – content that disappears after a short period. This trend capitalizes on FOMO (Fear Of Missing Out) and encourages frequent engagement due to the fleeting nature of the content.

11. Marketing Automation: Marketing automation tools are streamlining repetitive tasks, enabling marketers to focus on strategic initiatives. Automated email campaigns, personalized recommendations, and lead nurturing are becoming more efficient and effective.

12. Predictive Analytics : Predictive analytics leverage historical data to forecast future trends and consumer behaviors. This empowers marketers to make informed decisions and allocate resources more effectively, ultimately leading to improved campaign outcomes.

The future of marketing is being shaped by a multitude of interconnected trends that reflect the changing landscape of consumer behavior and technological capabilities.

Conclusion

In the dynamic realm of business, where success is the ultimate pursuit, mastering the intricate dance of marketing is the key to unlock unprecedented achievements. Just as an artist wields a brush to create a masterpiece, a marketer employs the Marketing Mastery Code to craft a symphony that resonates with the audience, leaving an indelible mark on their hearts and minds.

Simplifying Success: The Marketing Mastery Code illuminates the path to triumph in a world inundated with choices, information, and noise. In this era of constant connectivity, where every business vies for attention, the essence of success lies in cutting through the clutter and forging a genuine connection. The Marketing Mastery Code is the compass that guides modern marketers, enabling them to navigate the complex landscape with finesse.

As we delve into the labyrinth of marketing strategies, the first revelation is the power of simplicity. The age-old adage "less is more" holds true as we witness the impact of clear and concise messaging. The Code reminds us that complexity breeds confusion, while simplicity invites comprehension. By distilling intricate concepts into easily digestible forms, marketers can capture attention swiftly and etch their message into the collective consciousness.

Moreover, the Code underscores the importance of empathy in the pursuit of success. In an era where consumers seek authenticity and connection, understanding their needs and aspirations is paramount. By stepping into the shoes of the audience, marketers can tailor their campaigns to resonate on a personal level. The Code teaches us that success is not merely measured in sales figures, but in the lasting relationships nurtured through empathetic engagement.

In the digital age, data is hailed as the new currency. The Marketing Mastery Code elucidates the art of harnessing data to drive decision-making. From analyzing consumer behavior to tracking the efficacy of campaigns, data provides invaluable insights. The Code emphasizes that success lies not only in gathering data, but in interpreting it to extract meaningful conclusions. This fusion of art and science empowers marketers to refine their strategies iteratively, inching closer to the zenith of success.

As we ascend the ladder of success, the Code reminds us that adaptability is non-negotiable. In a landscape that evolves at a dizzying pace, rigidity spells obsolescence. Marketers who embrace change, experiment with novel approaches, and embrace innovation are the torchbearers of triumph. The Code inspires us to view challenges as opportunities for growth and to pivot when necessary, ensuring that our strategies remain aligned with the ever-shifting tides of the market.

The ultimate revelation encapsulated within the Marketing Mastery Code is that success is not a solitary endeavor, but a symphony conducted by collaboration. In a hyper-connected world, partnerships foster synergies that propel brands to new heights. The Code champions the art of building networks, nurturing alliances, and co-creating with others. Through collaboration, marketers pool their collective genius, amplifying their impact and transcending individual limitations.

In conclusion, Simplifying Success: The Marketing Mastery Code encapsulates the quintessence of triumph in a world where marketing is the bridge between brands and consumers. From the power of simplicity to the importance of empathy, from data-driven insights to the spirit of adaptability, and from individual brilliance to collaborative excellence, the Code unravels the multifaceted tapestry of success.

As we stand at the crossroads of the present and the future, armed with the wisdom imparted by the Code, we are poised to redefine success. By adhering to its principles, we embrace the transformative journey from obscurity to prominence, from insignificance to eminence. The Code is not merely a guide; it is the anthem of the modern marketer, resonating across boardrooms and brainstorming sessions, shaping strategies and steering brands toward the zenith of success. So, let us inscribe the teachings of the Marketing Mastery Code into our marketing lexicon and embark on a voyage where success is not a destination, but an exhilarating odyssey.

www.ingramcontent.com/pod-product-compliance
Lightning Source LLC
Chambersburg PA
CBHW062351290526
45794CB00005B/2174